Restore Joy to Your Life

28 Suggestions for Renewing Your Mind

Greg Gerber

Faithfire Media
PO Box 2474
Sun City, AZ 85372
602.586.5535 | info@faithfiremedia.com

Copyright © 2020 by Greg Gerber

ALL RIGHTS RESERVED. This book contains material protected under international and federal copyright laws and treaties. Any unauthorized reprint or use of this material is prohibited. No part of this book may be reproduced or transmitted in any form or by any means, electronic or mechanical, including photocopying, recording or by any information storage and retrieval system, without the express written permission from the author or publisher.

ISBN:

PREFACE

Everyone gets in a slump from time to time.

However, I spent years experiencing little joy in my life. It seemed that I was buried under a never-ending pile of problems.

Have you ever watched a football player fumble a ball? One hefty player after another piles on. The weight at the bottom must be crushing. After a while, your problems can feel the same way.

When you are in that type of situation, it is hard to find any joy in your life.

This booklet is written from a Christian perspective. In it, you'll find some Bible quotes. However, the information is designed to help anyone find more joy in their lives.

I'll try not to preach, but just know that I found joy when I found faith. And I experienced more joy when I implemented these suggestions.

The list is compiled from my own experiences and those of people I know. I conducted some research on what has worked for others as well, and I've pored over journals I've written and notes I have gathered over the years.

My goal has been to create a booklet that is easy to read without overwhelming you with information. My hope is that you'll find value in at least one of these suggestions.

Life is way too short to live a joyless existence. I want you to live life to the full.

I suspect you want that, too.

INTRODUCTION

According to the National Institute of Mental Health (NIMH), one out of every fourteen people suffers from severe clinical depression.

That type of depression needs to be treated by trained professionals through medication and counseling. It's nothing to ignore. Failing to address clinical depression can be deadly. Seek help now!

For the rest of us, we often go through periods of doubt, depression, sadness and a general funk. Dictionary.com defines a slump as a period during which a person performs slowly, inefficiently or ineffectively; or to sink heavily as in spirit. We may or may not know the cause, but it's real.

It can suck the joy right out of your life. When I am in a slump, it's hard to see any light at all. The darkness seems to feed off itself. The more I dwell in darkness, the darker life becomes. NIMH notes that more than one in four people who experienced strokes become depressed. That included me.
I had a minor stroke in September 2018. It took

more than six months to clear that feeling of depression. I was moody, hopeless, and angry. I was no fun to be around, and I saw impending doom around every corner.

Yet, when you're surrounded by darkness, even the smallest light can be seen for quite a distance. LiveScience.com reports the average person can see about three miles on a flat surface in daylight. But, get on top of a hill, and you can see a candle flicker from thirty miles away.

Have you ever attended a candlelight church service on Christmas Eve? The most incredible memory I have is attending a church that seated several thousand people. It was much bigger than a movie theater.

Once the lights were turned off, the pastor lit a match. It was instantly visible. With the match, he lit a candle. He used that candle to light one other one, and that person turned and lit still another candle.

As the candles lit up, the room brightened until it was possible to see every corner of the auditorium—and every person in it—as clear as day.

If we can find one source of light and nurture it enough, we'll produce more light. We will soon be enveloped in a feeling of joy and contentment.

But, where to find that spark? This booklet provides twenty-eight ideas on ways you can find joy. Try implementing one each day—or week—and watch how the spring returns to your step and you become more enthusiastic about life.

Caution: it will take some work on your part. These suggestions will require effort, either in changing your thinking or in avoiding people and situations that bring you down and keep you down.

By reading through these ideas, you'll see things that actively reduce joy in your life. Eliminate them and you'll work to fertilize the small seeds of joy you do plant in your mind. Eventually, you will reap a harvest of godly fruit, including love, joy, peace, patience, kindness, goodness, faithfulness, gentleness and self-control.

Turn Off Online News

One of the biggest excuses I hear for keeping a television on in a home is the need to stay abreast of current events. Online news, however, is often worse than TV and print news for several reasons.

First, it is constantly updated. You don't have to wait for the paper or evening news broadcast to get the news. That also means that news is sometimes released without proper vetting, and only corrected later.

News junkies can get addicted to online news. Then they spend a lot of time getting a fix, which just makes them sadder, angrier, and more depressed.

The media is profit-motivated to keep you outraged so that you keep coming back for more updates. Don't fall for that type of mind control.

Here's the reality. Beyond voting, you likely can't do a single thing to change the situation. It is out of your control. So, why should you invest one-minute being outraged about something you can't fix?

I was a news junkie, and still am in some regards. But, I have found a resource that keeps me abreast of what's happening without requiring me to delve into the nitty gritty details and endless commentary.

Check out www.disrn.com and subscribe to the free daily newsletter. Every morning, you can scan headlines and click through to get three to five paragraphs of additional information and the original source.

You'll be able to know what's happening without having to invest hours wading through the muck of what has become journalism today.

Stop reading news comments

If your civic duty won't allow you to turn off the news completely, then do whatever you can to turn off the comments to news stories or avoid reading them.

These snarky, mean, anonymous comments don't contribute a single thing to any news story. People making comments will belittle others, pass judgement on them, and say things online that they would never tell someone to their face—ever.

Most of the people making these comments are ill-informed or simply commenting on something taken way out of context from the original story.

The comments section is not an online debate with both sides bringing evidence to support their arguments. Online comments are rude, crass, profane, slanderous, and libelous.

If you like the topic, comments work to reinforce what you already believe. If you don't like the topic, then comments simply reinforce your outrage.

Remember, you can't do one thing about the situation. Plus, with their 24-hour news cycles, the media needs to keep you outraged. They are very much like drug dealers who give you just a taste of what you crave in order to force you to return frequently just to get another fix.

Turn off the news and pick up a book instead.

Thomas Jefferson once said that a person who never reads a book is more educated than someone who only reads the newspaper. That is still true today.

Turn Off the Television Completely

In 2014, I bought a motorhome and began a three year cross-country journey living and working full time from the RV.

I was working as a journalist covering the recreation vehicle industry. So I traveled around interviewing people working in the industry and using its products.

While the motorhome had two televisions, what it didn't have was an antenna capable of picking up over-the-air signals unless the tower was very close to the RV.

As a result, I stopped watching television all together. No more TV news. No more sports. No more foul-mouthed late-night "comedy" hosts. No more disgusting shows masquerading as entertainment.

I only had access to cellular data, so I couldn't even stream programs into my RV because it was too cost-prohibitive.

For years, I bought DVDs on sale and accumulated nearly four hundred movies and documentaries. Those became my sole source of entertainment. I would often watch a different movie every night.

Breaking my bondage to television was much easier than I expected. In a matter of days, I didn't miss commercial television one iota.

Prior to that, I was pretty much addicted to television entertainment. But, I was frustrated with all the commercials. I read a story the other day that noted some TV stations now broadcast only eighteen minutes of programming every half hour. The rest of the time promotes commercial messages.

I didn't consider it entertaining in the least to be bombarded with commercials about one "must-have" product after another. Yet, some people even pay cable and satellite companies more than a hundred dollars per month to have nearly non-stop commercials pushed into their homes.

Here's the truth: you are not "missing out" if you don't know who is sleeping with whom on your favorite drama. You won't feel a hole in your heart if you don't get the opportunity to "relax" to some foul-mouthed comedic tirade before bed.

The reality of your life is infinitely better than the best scripted "reality" on display in any TV show. Unplugging from television is likely the fastest way to restore joy to your life.

Turn Your Car
Into A University

Another way to renew your mind is to control what you put into it. Rather than listen to a talk show or politicized sports show, turn it off and turn your car audio system into a university.

There are literally thousands of audio books about every conceivable topic. I frequently use Audible to download a variety of books. Learn to start a business, grow a garden, improve your prayer time, plan a vacation, strengthen your faith, or improve your mental attitude.

You can improve your business skills, your interpersonal skills, your financial prowess, or even learn how to invest—you know, everything you should have learned in high school.

What about reading all those classic books that you've always wanted to read, or the book your favorite movie is based on? If you don't have time to read, then listen to them instead.

My favorite things to listen to are motivational messages by some of the most gifted and talented speakers in the world. My favorites are Zig Ziglar, Napoleon Hill, and Og Mandino.

Biographies are great, too. I find them encouraging because they tell the story behind the story. Rarely is someone a genuine overnight success. He or she may achieve overnight fame, but there is often incredible work and sacrifice that went into preparing the person to become an "overnight success." I find those stories to be inspirational.

Faith-based books are great for reminding you of who you are, who you were created to be, and for providing help in other areas of your life.

With audiobooks, you can listen to a Bible study and increase your understanding of various chapters, authors, stories, people or cultures of the time. Not only will it make the Bible come alive, you will greatly improve your understanding of that life-changing book.

Do you like to travel? With audiobooks, you can go anywhere in the world to learn about a culture, destinations and attractions, the history of the area, and famous people who came from that state or country.

Just be careful when selecting an audiobook. You don't want to turn off television news only to give some political pundit access to your mind for several hours at a time.

Check out my website at
www.greggerber.com/resources
for a list of my favorite books.

Unfollow, Unfriend and Block

Social media is a wonderful tool for staying in touch with friends, family and acquaintances. But, just like the comments on news stories, some posts and comments on social forums can get under your skin and work to steal your joy.

One of the best features about social media is the ability to unfriend, unfollow, and outright block people who routinely get on your nerves.

If you haven't figured it out already, I abhor politics for its negativity. When I log onto social media, I want to see happy pictures of people having fun. I want to share the joy of a new baby, new pet, engagement, promotion, well-earned vacation, new car, a family beginning an RV adventure, or even a funny joke . . .

I don't want to view Conspiracy Charlie's latest missive about whatever has him boiling today. Nor do I need to see Dreadful Donna's post about how she expects this or that bad thing to ruin everyone's life.

If the same people keep posting things that you don't agree with—or worse, if they hijack your own posts to inject their negative attitude into the comments—then you don't have to put up with that.

If you don't really know these people well, open their profile and click the "Unfriend" button. You certainly don't need any more negative people in your life. Period. There is no law that says you must accept every friend request that comes your way.

Unfortunately, if you unfriend close friends or relatives, you may incur their wrath later. Thankfully, Facebook and other social media platforms have created a relationship-saving tool to help.

Just visit the their profile and click the "Unfollow" button. It works just like blocking in that you'll never see any of their posts again. Best of all, they'll never know that you've kicked them to the curb. As far as they are concerned, you're still their friend and they think you're benefiting from the crap they share with the world.

If, upon occasion, they actually post something that really matters, you can visit their profile and scroll down to find that once-a-month happy post. But, you consume the content on your terms, when you want it rather than having it thrust before you every time you log on to a social media site.

If you ever get cornered by Negative Nancy asking what you thought of her most recent Facebook rant, you can honestly shrug your shoulders and claim you never saw it. After all, you're busy and you can't control the algorithms that determine what you see, right?

Just promise to check it out right away so you don't get trapped into listening to that nonsense at that moment.

One of the best ways I discovered to see more positive posts is to like everything you see along those lines.

For me, I like faith-based memes and scripture verses. So, by liking them when they cross my newsfeed, I train the Facebook robots to believe that I want to see more of them.

I also found a wonderful tool that has saved my Facebook experience. It's called Fluff Busting Purity.

It's a free extension for Chrome and Firefox that truly filters what you see on Facebook.

Facebook doesn't like it because you take control over what you get to see rather than allowing some algorithm to control your content.

It bugs me that Facebook seems driven to display a new ad after every five posts. FB Purity can block those, too.

I can also set the app to block various keywords for posts I don't want to see. It's not smart enough to detect those keywords in images, like memes, but I can block posts that contain those words. I set the app to block any post that contains the words Republican, Democrat, Trump, Obama, Clinton, etc.

You do have to be careful when using the blocking feature, because setting it to block "Warren" would also block news of relatives talking about their kids' achievements at Warren High School, not just posts about a presidential candidate.

Play around with the app and see how it brings joy back into your Facebook experience.

Remove Toxic People

There are people in all our lives who seem to make it a mission to hunt down and destroy any joy we might have (or want to have) in our lives.

These people are often deeply wounded themselves. They are the first to make snarky comments on social media posts. When they walk into a room, the lights dim as all positive energy is sucked out.

There is an old saying that you will become like the five people you associate with the most. You certainly don't want a toxic relationship stealing joy from your life.

Don't accept a lunch or dinner invitation from a toxic person. If you must meet with those people regularly, then set boundaries that put certain topics off limits. If they don't comply with your request, there is nothing that requires you to sit there and listen to that junk.

Do you get together every week to play cards knowing it will devolve into another negative event where people bash their spouses, bosses, neighbors, and coworkers? You don't need to participate in those gripe fests, either.

Start your own card group, game night, or team, and invite only those people who will make it fun.

Stop attending negative gatherings and giving people permission to draw you into their problems. Remember, it's not your circus, not your monkeys, and certainly not your problem.

Yes, everyone gets in a situation from time to time where he or she gets overwhelmed and just needs a good friend to listen and offer advice. As that type of friend, you'll want to support others during times of trouble or frustration.

But when it's chronic complaining about the same problems, time and time again—with no effort to make any reasonable changes—then pack up and move on. If nothing changes, then nothing changes. Make excuses to stop meeting with those people.

Trust me, they will eventually find someone else to listen to their tripe.

A word about abusive spouses.

As a Christian, I truly believe that a marriage should last a lifetime. I grew up in a single-parent home and only saw my father six times a year. The Bible says God hates divorce because he knows the impact it can have on people, especially children.

However, I did not practice what I preach, and I wound up divorced twenty-six years and one day after I got married. (That could be the topic of another book.)

But, if you are being abused, or your children are being abused, God does not intend for you to go on living in that situation. Get out of it—fast!

Yes, it's possible to make a mistake when someone's anger overtakes him or her in a stressful situation. It is still not an excuse for abusive behavior. God tells us to turn the other cheek and forgive people. However, God doesn't expect you to be a punching bag for some bully, or to be a doormat for a someone else to walk over every day. To believe that is bad theology.

Pray earnestly for the situation. Seek professional counseling, if your spouse is willing to participate. If the marriage can be saved, you and your children will be better off in the long run. But you do not have to endure abuse. Flee that situation.

Watch Your Words

I could spend the rest of my life studying how the brain works, especially the subconscious mind, and never fully understand its power.

But I have spent enough time in personal observation and in reading the research of others to know that you attract whatever you dwell upon. That's why watching your words is so vitally important.

Tell yourself, "I think I'm getting sick," and your brain will kick into overdrive, looking for things to confirm that notion. You'll notice other people sneezing and coughing. Soon, you will be legitimately sick.

Tell your mind that you feel great and are glad to be alive, and your subconscious will look for reasons to reaffirm that, too.

One of the best books ever written is *Hung by the Tongue* by Francis P. Martin. Written in 1976, it is a timeless classic on how self-talk can guide your destiny. At ninety-two pages, it's a short read and available at just about any library. You can also listen to it free on YouTube.

It will change the way you look at the words you speak—especially the words you tell yourself. Be very, very careful telling yourself, "I'm an idiot," or "I can't do this." Using words like "never" intentionally cements your mind to believe that. All your mind wants to do is please you. So, whatever you think about will surely come to pass.

One of my favorite sayings, apparently written long ago, is this:

> Two natures beat within my breast;
> One is foul, the other blessed.
> One I love, the other I hate.
> The one I feed will dominate.

Tell yourself you hate your job, spouse or life, and you'll soon see ample evidence to support that conclusion. Remind yourself how grateful you are for the job, how much your spouse has helped you, and how many blessings you already enjoy, and soon you'll be overwhelmed with those thoughts.

It's almost magical. Many consider the tongue to be a force of nature.

Proverbs 18:20-21 says,

"From the fruit of their mouth a person's stomach is filled; with the harvest of their lips they are satisfied. The tongue has the power of life and death, and those who love it will eat its fruit."

Frank Outlaw, the former president of Bi-Lo Stores, once wrote:

Watch your thoughts, for they become words.
Watch your words, for they become actions.
Watch your actions, for they become habits.
Watch your habits, for they become character.
Watch your character, for it becomes your destiny.

Your destiny is impacted more by your words than you realize. They'll become fertilizer for whatever your mind hears.

Read The Bible

I need to be careful here. I truly believe you should always read the Bible and you should do it from cover to cover as part of an organized plan or established study.

The Bible is an outstanding source of wisdom, encouragement and personal insight. The Psalms and Proverbs are two of my favorite go-to books in the Bible whenever I am feeling blue and just need to be reminded of who God is, what he thinks of me, and what his plan is for my life.

However, reading parts of the Bible can be anything but uplifting. With all its rules, talk of war, warnings of judgement, and endless litany of problems, some books of the Old Testament can be hard to read and understand in context with the rest of scripture.

I encourage people to spend time in the Gospels, the first four books of the New Testament. The books of Matthew, Mark, Luke and John are excellent resources for renewing your mind because they quote Jesus' own words.

If you truly want to change your attitude and restore joy to your life, really study the New Testament. In it, Jesus outlines the new covenant he made with his followers that goes far beyond the rules and traditions of religion.

You'll find tons of golden nuggets of truth within those pages. Pause and mediate on those—plus Psalms and Proverbs—and you'll do a lot to restore joy to our soul.

Better yet, join an organized Bible study or invite another Christian to join you for coffee to delve into a book of the Bible or a specific topic.

The search function in online Bible apps is an excellent tool for finding God's word on just about any topic.

The YouVersion app offers a ton of free short-term Bible studies as well as free Bibles you can download to your smartphone. Just pick a version that speaks to your heart in language you can understand.

A lot of people enjoy the King James version, but I find the formal Old English wording to be distracting. A bunch of folks like the simplicity found in The Message version. Many churches recommend the New Living Translation.

Personally, I have used the New International Version for decades. The only disappointing aspect of that version is that the publishers feel compelled to change the wording as more research is done into translations.

The good news is that there is no right or wrong version. One is sure to speak to your heart.

To get an idea of what version would work best for you, visit biblegateway.com. In the search bar, enter John 1 and click Search. It will bring up that book in the default version. However, you can click on the version to select one of dozens of different Bible types. You can even click to have it read to you.

The Bible is a special book. Hebrews 4:12 says, "For the word of God is alive and active. Sharper than any double-edged sword, it penetrates even to dividing soul and spirit, joints and marrow; it judges the thoughts and attitudes of the heart."

You can't read the Bible without being changed, challenged, or encouraged in some way. Spending just fifteen minutes a day reading the Bible will surprise you in how much your attitude improves.

Volunteer

One of the best, most enduring ways to bring joy to your life is to serve other people. And, when you do it for free, it brings joy to your heart.

The need for volunteer workers is high in every community in the world. Here's a partial list of places seeking short-term volunteer positions:

- Schools—Monitoring cafeterias and playgrounds, reading to children, tutoring students, serving as a classroom aide, and shelving books.

- Senior centers—Running errands for residents, assembling puzzles, delivering meals, preparing biographies for seniors to pass on to family, helping fill out tax forms, fixing things for seniors, teaching classes (how to use a cell phone is a popular topic), helping them with chores, or just engaging people in conversation.

- Animal shelters—Walking dogs, cuddling abandoned or sick pets, cleaning cages, or simply talking to the animals so they don't feel neglected or abandoned.

- Homeless and abuse shelters—Preparing meals, playing games with clients, or hosting a party for kids celebrating birthdays that month
- Churches—Getting ready for services, rocking babies, preparing weekly bulletins or mailings, cleaning, performing yard work, teaching a class, leading a small group of people who desire to share life, or helping people overcome problems you've already faced.
- Federal, state, county and local parks—Picking up trash, performing lawn care or trail maintenance, cleaning campgrounds, conducting tours of historical sites, and staffing gates or welcome desks.
- Food pantries and clothing donation centers—Sorting donations, pricing items, or serving customers.

You don't even need to be part of an organization to volunteer. Raking leaves, shoveling snow, or mowing grass for an elderly or disabled neighbor serves several purposes. First, it provides a needed service. Second, you'll get to know someone from your neighborhood in the process.

Are there any single moms in your area? They might need help watching kids, making repairs, preparing a meal, or shuttling kids to activities.

(When working with or around kids, take steps to protect yourself from accusations by not being alone with a child or being overly physical with him or her.)

Has someone been sick at home, lost a relative, lost a job, been recently divorced, or moved into the area? A hot meal, pizza, container of cookies—even flowers and a visit—can brighten their day and yours.

Help someone pack or unpack. Who couldn't use an extra set of hands and a little friendly conversation when going through the hassle of moving?

Truly, there are countless ways to serve other people and make yourself feel good in the process.

I like to do secret work, like cleaning a bathroom at a busy gas station, clearing tables at an understaffed restaurant, and by picking up trash along the road or sidewalk.

Is there a tourist attraction in your area? Simply hang out and offer to take pictures of families so Mom or Dad can get in on the memories.

Here are a few websites with creative opportunities for volunteering:

- https://blog.prepscholar.com/129-examples-of-community-service-projects
- https://blog.fundly.com/community-service-ideas

Here's one for kids and adults:

- https://lancaster.unl.edu/4h/serviceideas.shtml

Turn Off Your Phone

This is a problem of our own making. We invite a beast into our lives—and pay a lot of money for it—just to have it beep, sing and vibrate every time someone feels they have an urgent message to share with us.

If you were born before 1990, you probably remember the good old days when if you didn't want to talk to anyone, you just took the phone off the hook or unplugged the cord from the back of the phone.

Thank God for voicemail.

Just because the phone rings does not mean you have to answer it that moment. Chances are extraordinarily high it is a spam call or robocall anyway. So, ignore it.

I set up my phone so that four people can call me any time of day or night. They are my mother and three daughters.

For everyone else, it is highly unlikely that something is a truly life-and-death situation that requires your immediate attention. So, let the calls go to voicemail and respond when it's convenient for you.

I set up time zones on my business phone line to regulate when calls can come through. If the call comes through outside of those times, they get to talk to voicemail.

At the time of this writing, there are apps being developed that will intercept every call coming into your cell phone. If the caller's number is in your contact list, the phone will either ring through or go to voicemail depending upon how you have it set up.

If the contact isn't on your phone, the app hangs up the call without you even knowing that it came in. You don't even get a robocall voice message telling you that the IRS is going to "call the cops" if you don't immediately address a non-existent problem with your taxes.

As you introduce more silence into your life, you will discover more joy returning as well.

It's not just phone calls that work to compete for your attention. With games and internet access available on the phone, it can suck up your attention—even when you're with others.

Now, I am the first to admit that it is nice to be able to look up an answer in the middle of a conversation, if clarification is needed. What was the name of that Tom Hanks movie where he was stranded on a deserted island? Both you and whomever you are talking to won't get any rest until you find the answer.

However, if you want to see just how addicted people are to their phones, go to any sit-down restaurant and walk through the rows of tables. If half the people aren't on their phones, or have a phone at their fingertips, stop and take a picture. It's not a sight you see that often.

Turn Off Phone Notifications

This is the evil twin of cell phone use. To bring joy back into your life, you need to reduce the number of distractions competing for your attention.

Cell phones are appropriately named because they often keep us in cells as prisoners to the whims of others. The notifications are endless:

- Someone posts something to social media—beep.
- Someone comments on a post you made—beep.
- Someone sends you a text message—beep.
- Or worse, someone includes you on a group text—beep, beep, beep, beep, beep.
- An app releases a new feature—beep.
- The pizza place down the street is offering $2 off if you order right this second—beep.
- There is a breaking news story—beep.
- Your credit card statement is available—beep.
- Your dentist is reminding you of an appointment tomorrow—beep.
- Someone sends you a picture of their puppy or grandkids—beep.

These squirrels are killing your joy!

It got to the point that I shut off notifications for every single app on my phone except for my bank, calendar appointments, and apps I use for travel, like Southwest Airlines (to get flight updates) and Uber (to confirm a ride).

You really need to be diligent about turning off apps, too. I can't tell you how many times I have downloaded a new app only to have it start spewing out messages promoting some special offer until I shut off those notifications.

Don't fool yourself either. Just turning off the sound doesn't work. Whenever you see that blinking light, it works to shout, "Squirrel!" and distract you from what's really important.

Support and Encourage Others

If you ever find yourself in a funk, there is a surefire way to restore joy to your soul. It is so effective that you'll ever wonder why you allowed yourself to remain down in the past.

All you need to do is reach out to offer support, encouragement or an uplifting word to others.

Something about it works to rewire your brain to think more positive thoughts.

My daughter, Rebecca, is a master at sending handwritten notecards to people at random. It might be to thank them for a gift, offer congratulations or just offer some encouragement.

Her notes are keepers. They are filled with positive affirmation. You can't help but feel special when you receive one of her notes. She keeps a stack of notecards handy just to be ready to spread a little joy or sunshine into the lives of others.

How does that help restore joy to your life? It works like magic in several ways.

First, when you are writing words of encouragement, you are thinking about those words and often reciting them silently (or even verbally) as you write them out. That works to reprogram your brain.

Second, it is impossible for your mind to harbor a positive and negative thought at the same time. So, by focusing on positive words, you are shooing away negative thoughts at the same time.

You don't need notecards to enjoy the same effect. It also works with email and even social media, provided you don't get caught up in all the negatives associated with that platform.

It's very easy to get started. Try it yourself.

Grab a pen and a notecard, or open an email window, and start writing:

- Hi Mary, I just want you to know that I've been thinking a lot about you and how much I appreciate our friendship because . . .

- Tom, I was just thinking about you and that time we took a trip on your boat. I will never forget how much we laughed when you did . . .
- Mr. Larson, I don't think I ever told you how much I appreciated the extra attention you gave me in English class when I was a junior. It changed my life and here's how . . .

You'll lighten your burden and give the gift of a smile to someone else. Everyone loves to receive a fun email or handwritten note. Do this and the joy around you will spread like wildfire.

Make the Decision

One of the major contributors to anxiety or worry is the need to make a decision. The harder the choice to make, the more anxiety that seems to come with it.

However, the strangest thing happens once you make that decision. The anxiety evaporates as your mind begins to focus on why that was the best decision to make and how you're going to accomplish it.

There have been several times in my life where just the act of making a decision immediately brought joy to my life.

I really didn't like my job. It was stressful, a waste of my talent, demeaning, unrewarding, and taking me absolutely nowhere. I had wanted to do something else for a while, but worry always stood in the way. What would I do for income? Would I have to move to take a new job? Who would I be disappointing if I moved on?

I took a half-day off from work and went driving. Something compelled me to visit a city about thirty miles away. While driving around, I felt drawn to the university admission's office. I applied that day.

The next week, I quit my job with nothing lined up to replace it.

But a weight was lifted off my shoulders. I had a sense something would work out. The week I started school, I was offered a job that paid more than the stinking one I quit, and gave me the flexibility to attend classes and be a father.

When facing a major decision, the questions can seem overwhelming. The what-if scenarios playing out in your mind can appear daunting.

You expect the best, but imagine the worst.

Yet, when you make a decision, it is like the cloud evaporates and rays of sunshine pour in.

I remember fretting over a dating relationship I was in that really wasn't bringing me any joy. Yet, the moment I decided to end it, I instantly felt better.

The word "decide" is derived from the Latin word decidere, which literally means "to cut off." When you make a decision, you are cutting off or severing other options.

Not having other options allows your mind to focus on making the choice you selected a reality. You'll be impressed with how quickly clarity brings joy to your thinking.

Don't let other people make the decision for you or even give their opinion any thought. Seek God's opinion first. If he gives the green light, then jump in. He's already working three steps ahead of you.

The exception may be a decision that could seriously impact a child. For example, do you quit your job and move to a new city when your child will soon graduate from high school? If you're divorced, do you move so far away that your child may not see his mother or father?

Those are situations that require extra prayer and wise counsel of others.

But, for most decisions you've been putting off, suck it up and make the decision that your heart tells you is the best choice.

Create
A Thanksgiving List

It has been said that expressing gratitude is the easiest way to encounter peace and joy. I have found that to be the case indeed.

One day, I made a list of the hundred things I am most thankful for. It's harder than you think to come up with a hundred items! Consider these:

- Your health—Eyesight, having all your limbs, a working heart, and the ability to take a breath. Many people don't have those things we take for granted, so be thankful for them.

- Favorite foods—For me, oatmeal raisin cookies and a glass of milk should be their own food group. I could eat a supreme pizza every day. Don't get me started on beer brats. And sorry, but nothing beats an In-N-Out Double-Double hamburger.

- Places you visited—List trips you have enjoyed, cities you lived in, and schools you attended.

- Things you possess—A working car, a phone, a dishwasher, a microwave, a TV with a DVD player, a vacuum cleaner. Look in all those boxes you've hidden away in storage, too. You might be surprised to find something you'd forgotten about. At the very least, you'll have the impetus to toss a lot of the baggage you've been carting around for years.

- Simple luxuries—A hot shower, comfortable bed, heated or air-conditioned home, and running water. These are things many people in the world wish they had. I attended a conference once where the speaker was describing what it took to live among the top ten percent of all people in South Africa.

Those items included:

- DVD or Blu-ray player
- Refrigerator or combined fridge/freezer
- Electric stove
- Running tap water in house
- Microwave oven
- Flush toilet inside house
- Free-standing deep freezer
- Hot running water
- A washing machine
- Built-in kitchen sink
- A tumble dryer

- - Dishwasher
  - Cable TV
  - Mobile phone
  - Home theater system
  - Vacuum cleaner
  - One motor vehicle per household
  - Either a desktop or laptop computer

- Awards, honors and recognition—Things that made you feel accomplished and worthy. I am an Eagle Scout, and have received some writing awards. I also achieved magna cum laude in college and missed summa cum laude by .015 points as a father of three after getting a B in a one-credit sex education class. (I said we needed more home-study labs.)

- Unique experiences—Things you have done that few other people have had an opportunity to do. For me, it was going to the top of the Wisconsin state capitol dome, meeting the prime minister of Canada in the rotunda of the U.S. Capitol, living and working in a motorhome full time for three years, and visiting forty-nine states. (I'm holding out on going to Hawaii until I can go with someone special.)

Double your joy, and the challenge, by creating a separate list of the hundred people who have had the most impact on your life. Be sure to include:

- Long-time friends who always seem to be available to help when needed.
- Special friends who walked with you through a season in your life.
- Teachers who took an interest in your success.
- Coaches who helped you achieve more than you thought was possible.
- Early bosses who taught you skills you use today.
- People who taught you lessons you didn't want to learn, but are glad you did.
- Chance encounters that altered your destiny.
- Coworkers who made a job even more fun.
- Mentors who pushed you to achieve more, or helped open doors for you.
- Someone who introduced you to a hobby you enjoy today.

Whenever you find yourself feeling down, simply review those lists.

An attitude of gratitude will always work to restore joy to your spirit.

Journal Thoughts

I'll admit that I am prone to being rather short-tempered from time to time. Combine that with the ability to speak and write very well, and I can become a human flamethrower if I'm not careful.

Oh, how I wish I could go back in time to retrieve words spoken or written in anger and frustration!

While I might have felt better after venting, that feeling was short-lived (if I had it at all). Destroying someone else is no way to bring joy to your life.

Revenge doesn't work either.

But, it's not a good idea to pent up that anger or frustration. If you do that, it just eats away at your mind, mood and soul. Then you can't stop dwelling upon the injustice of whatever happened.

That hurt must come out somehow, but in a healthy way. So, try this to bring joy back to your life.

Get a notebook and start writing. Fill up one page after another. Spill your guts. Express your anger. Explain how hurt you were by the insensitivity of a friend or how you were treated by a company.

Tell your boss exactly what you think about him as a person. If you want to bring his mother into the conversation, now is the time to do it.

Don't hold back. Let that insensitive, cruel, selfish oaf know exactly what you think.

Then, set down the pen and take a break. Think about the situation some more. When you're ready to start writing again, start with the words, "And another thing . . ."

Get it all out.

Then sit on it for a week. Better yet, put it in an envelope, attach a stamp and mail it to yourself. Just be careful someone can't intercept the mail when it arrives.

The act of getting it off your chest and out of your mind will help bring joy back to your life.

It won't change anything, because nothing has really changed. You'll still need to confront the problem if you want genuine resolution.

However, once you're done venting, you will be able to approach the situation more calmly. With your mind clear of anger or hatred, you'll be in a better position to see a solution.

In the days after you've privately vented, perhaps God will give you insight you didn't have before. Maybe your friend reacted the way he did because his mom is really sick and his mind is focused on her welfare.

Could it be your boss came down hard on you because his boss is coming down hard on him? When you're calm, you can both strategize a way to remedy the situation.

Maybe your teenage daughter erupted for the fourth time today because she's being bullied at school or harassed online, and she feels powerless to do anything about it.

The key to a joyful life is to learn that how to vent your own anger in a way that doesn't destroy another person.

Forgive Others and Forgive Yourself

Unforgiveness is like a poison you drink in hopes of it hurting other people. When you can't forgive yourself for past mistakes, it creates a cloud of darkness that follows you wherever you go.

I don't know of a single person who has lived a perfect life, who hasn't either been on the receiving end of some horrific abuse or made a mess of a good thing.

In 2009, I was at one of the lowest points of my life and depression had set in. One thing that really brought me out of it—almost instantly—was forgiving people who had hurt me. It was astonishing how much baggage I had been carrying around for years.

One night, I had enough. I sat down and made a list of every person I could remember who had hurt me, betrayed me, or somehow taken advantage of me.

I included everyone from my father who abandoned me, to the bully in seventh grade who broke my arm. I added the boss who fired me for the silliest of reasons, the teacher who made snide personal remarks about my ability, and the pastor who humiliated me in front of dozens of people.

I must have had a list of nearly one hundred people I needed to forgive.

Then, alone with God, one after another, I recalled out loud what had happened and how much it hurt me. After speaking about the pain of the circumstance, I announced that I forgave that person.

Next, I turned the spotlight on myself. I made a list of the things I had done that I knew had hurt others. I added those times I had truly let down a good friend, recalled people I mistreated, and thought about promises I made which I knew I had broken.

I confessed what I had done and asked God to forgive me and heal the heart of the person I had wronged.

I was exhausted when I was finished, but my heart was free. I enjoyed the soundest night's sleep I had experienced in many years.

When I woke up, it was as though I was in a whole new world. I wish I could have bottled that feeling! Today, I keep a short list and forgive people as quickly as I am offended. There is no need to allow that dark cloud to follow me.

It worked wonders. I said I had a list of one hundred people I needed to forgive, but today, I can only recall a handful of those experiences. The other hurts have vanished from my memory.

Laugh out Loud

There is an old saying that laughter is the best medicine, and it's right. It's very hard to remain sullen after you've had a belly laugh.

Doctors will say that laughter forces you to breathe in lots of air, which adds oxygen to your blood. It also releases endorphins that tickle your pleasure points, much like getting a high.

For me, it's impossible to will myself into a laughing episode. I need something to tickle my funny bone.

So, I have several go-to movies that are sure to make me feel better. It's true, the language may not be ideal, and some scenes should probably have been eliminated. But the movies work to lighten my mood.

Here are some of my favorites:

- *National Lampoon's Christmas Vacation* with Chevy Chase
- *The Blues Brothers* with John Belushi and Dan Aykroyd

- *Arthur* with Dudley Moore
- *Aladdin* with Robin Williams
- *My Cousin Vinny* with Joe Pesci
- *Groundhog Day* with Bill Murray
- *Planes, Trains & Automobiles* with Steve Martin and John Candy
- *Coming to America* with Eddie Murphy
- *A Christmas Story* with Darren McGavin

It used to be that you could find very funny comedians on TV. But now, it seems that they can't be funny without dropping F-bombs every twelve words. So, you might have to go back in time to find truly funny shows.

Visit YouTube and look up episodes of The Tonight Show with Johnny Carson. He was so good at making people feel good that he often took credit for starting more pregnancies than anyone else.

There is an entire YouTube series titled "Kids Say the Darndest Things." The children are so honest in expressing themselves that I can't help but laugh.

Good satire also works well to get me laughing. I love The Babylon Bee, which is a conservative satirical website that skewers everyone. Their fake headlines often make me laugh so much that my eyes sweat.

Satirical authors, like Mark Twain, can get me chuckling, too. Here's a great quote from him:

"I promised myself that I'd cancel all other forms of recreation just to attend his funeral."

Have you ever felt that way? I know I have.

Enjoy a Musical

There is something about music that brings a smile to my face. But, musicals can really get my toes tapping and make me feel more joyful.

Here are my favorite musicals:

- *The Sound of Music* with Julie Andrews
- *The Wizard of Oz* with Judy Garland
- *Mary Poppins* with Julie Andrews and Dick Van Dyke
- *A Chorus Line* with Michael Douglas
- *Grease* with John Travolta and
- Olivia Netwton-John
- *Mamma Mia!* and *Mamma Mia! 2* with Amanda Seyfried and featuring songs of ABBA
- *White Christmas* with Bing Crosby and Danny Kaye
- *The Greatest Showman* with Hugh Jackman
- *High School Musical* with Zac Efron and Vanessa Anne Hudgens

Anything produced by Rogers and Hammerstein is sure to make you feel better after watching. They collaborated to create some of the most popular music of all time.

Just listening to music can push the clouds away. I have several go-to playlists of songs that I reach for when I feel down. Within an hour or two, the sadness often disappears.

I've found listening to music during a drive in the country does wonders for restoring my joy.
I was a weird child and teenager. While others liked rock and roll, I always felt drawn to showtunes and what others might call "elevator music."

I'll still listen to oldies from time to time—and Christmas music is always in season—yet, much of my music preference zeros in on Christian music.

That's especially true of old classic hymns. I used to despise those "ancient" songs. But compared to today's 7-Eleven worship music (seven words repeated eleven times), those old hymns speak directly to my heart to bring peace and assurance. Why? Because they are strongly based on God's word.

Watch Videos

When I am in a real funk, sometimes it helps to take my mind off the things of this world and refocus on things enjoyed by others.
Sometimes a good cry just flushes all the worry, concern, anger and frustration out of your system, making room for joy to rush in to fill the void.

YouTube offers a plethora of free, fun videos to watch whenever you need a pick-me-up. Here are some of the categories I have found bring joy to my heart. Just search for any of these keywords:

- Soldiers surprising people—The family has been separated as mom or dad served extended time overseas. So, you know the reunions are going to be joyful experiences. They're even more special when they're unannounced surprises. I dare you not to cry!
- Kids being surprised—They've wanted it, thought about it, and dreamed about it for years. So how do they react when they finally get it? Either with tears of disbelief or ecstatic joy. Either way, you're in for a heart-warming experience watching those videos.

- Kids learning they're going to be adopted—After years of uncertainty, the moment kids learn they finally have a forever home is a heartfelt experience.

- Children welcoming a new puppy—Whether it is a birthday present, Christmas present, or fulfillment of a long-desired wish, a puppy brings joy to kids. You can siphon some of that joy, too, by watching their reactions.

- Dogs being surprised—They say when a dog is separated from its humans, it never stops looking for them. When their people friends finally arrive home from vacation, college, military deployment, or any long separation, the pets' expressions of joy tell you everything you need to know about true love.

If you click one link, YouTube graciously suggests dozens of other similar videos to ensure you'll have plenty of things to warm your heart.

So, grab a box of tissue, click on the links, and open the door for joy to return to your life.

Just Dream

A lot of research has been done proving that you attract what you think about. If you think thoughts of gloom and despair, you seem to attract more of that. The opposite is also true.

If you focus on pleasant dreams, goals, and rewards, you'll attract ideas that will help you achieve them.

One of the first steps in setting that goal is to clearly define what you want, or what your reward will be. You can help move that visionary process along by collecting photos of what it is you desire most.

Is it a happy family? Then seek pictures of a happy family.

Is it a dream vacation to a tropical destination? Then photos of cruise ships and resorts will capture your attention.

It used to be that every house had dozens of magazines. People could clip pictures or stories about things they enjoyed or wanted to do. Is there anyone born before the year 2000 who doesn't remember the day the Christmas catalog arrived in the mail or was brought home from the store?

Perhaps that's why Americans are often so depressed. They forgot how to dream.

Even the Bible tells us to dream, for "faith is confidence in what we hope for and assurance about what we do not see" (Hebrews 11:1).

Yes, I know that applies to getting to heaven.

But, it also applies to envisioning what it is we would like to do. It stimulates our mind to thinking about those things and it brings us joy.

What are your favorite things to do?

- Is it a campfire by a lake or a walk in the woods?
- Is it driving in the countryside with the top down or the windows open?
- Is it warm chocolate chip cookies with a tall glass of milk?
- Is it basking at the beauty of a waterfall?
- Is it places that have special meaning in your life, such as grandma's house or your old elementary school?

- Is it writing a play, authoring a book, or directing a movie?
- Is it welcoming a puppy or a baby or a grandchild?
- Is it being debt-free?
- Is it owning a business of your own?

Write down those things that would bring you joy. Then seek pictures of those things that you can pop into a scrapbook or a digital photo album. Skim through those images from time to time to keep the dream alive.

What the heck? Save the picture on your computer desktop so you see it at least once every day.

Benjamin Franklin is said to have written, "Some people die at twenty-five and aren't buried until seventy-five."

Why is that? Because they've given up on their dreams. Do whatever you can to rekindle that dream, that vision for a better life, and that sense of purpose you felt called to fulfill. Dream big!

Confess Sins

One of the greatest joy-stealers of all time is unconfessed sin.

Your past mistakes keep gnawing at you, reminding you of things you did that you shouldn't have (or things you didn't do that you should have).

It creates a mental playground for Satan to bombard you with suggestions like these:

- You screwed up too badly.
- Nobody is as guilty, perverted, wrong, neglectful, mean, or nasty as you are.
- God can't possibly love you for what you did.
- You call yourself a Christian and act the way you did. A true Christian would never do anything like that!

There is nothing you have done that will cause God to love you any less.

He made humans. He knew their weaknesses. He knew they would fail. He loves them anyway.

And he loves you, too.

Here are a few Bible passages that assure us of God's love:

- Psalms 103:12 says, "As far as the east is from the west, so far has he removed our transgressions from us." (Why east from west? Because unlike north and south, there is no end to east and west.)
- Romans 8:38-39 says, "For I am convinced that neither death nor life, neither angels nor demons, neither the present nor the future, nor any powers, neither height nor depth, nor anything else in all creation, will be able to separate us from the love of God that is in Christ Jesus our Lord."

This is one of God's most enduring promises, and one I must recite over and over myself:

1 John 1:9 says, "If we confess our sins, he is faithful and just and will forgive us our sins and purify us from all unrighteousness."
The key is confessing our sins. It doesn't require any special words or unique posture. All it requires

is a sincere agreement that your action wasn't what God would have wanted you to do.

Because Jesus already paid the penalty for those sins, you don't need to do anything else to atone. If you want to involve someone else in your confession, that's fine, but it's not required. It's just a discussion you need to have with God.

The act of confession closes the gap you created when you sinned. God didn't leave you. You ran away from God and hid, just like Adam and Eve did in the Garden of Eden. They could run, but they couldn't hide. God came looking for them knowing full well what they had done.

Yes, there were consequences for their actions, just as you've likely felt already. Even if you deserved punishment and got away with something, the act of beating yourself up for a long time was punishment itself.

Look through Old Photographs

Many people have found that looking through old photographs is a good way to restore joy.

Flipping through albums (or the stockpile of images stored on your computer) is a trip back through time to relive celebrations, victories, vacations, and pleasant experiences with close friends, coworkers and family.

It surprises me how just spending a few minutes looking through old photos can often morph into an all-night ordeal. Those happy images are sure to put a smile on your face and joy in your heart.

Several years ago, when my daughters had all graduated from high school and were out on their own, we gathered for the last Christmas we would celebrate as a family. I was divorced within a year.

Yet, the day after Christmas, we brought out giant tubs of old photographs and memorabilia. For hours, we sat in a circle reliving the old memories and sharing stories that we had long forgotten about. More precisely, I learned of things the girls did when they were young that would have brought about my early demise—or theirs—if I'd known about it back then.

I had maintained a "memory box" for each of the girls from the day of their birth. They relished looking back at what happened when they were born and seeing evidence of their lives unfolding as they grew and matured.

After a day of fun remembrance, we went out to enjoy a nice dinner and continue sharing stories. Ask the girls today, and they'll likely remark how it was one of their favorite Christmas memories.

You might think this exercise would be counterproductive, since you'd have to relive memories of loved ones who have died or are no longer part of your life. But you'd be mistaken.

Actually, seeing their photos sparks happy memories of the times you were able to share together. As Christians, we know we will be reunited with them soon enough.

If the person is still alive, perhaps seeing their picture will prompt a long-overdue phone call to catch up and remember the past. That kind of joy is contagious.

What about people who have brought you pain? How would seeing their pictures bring you joy?

Memory can be a demanding master, tying you to thoughts of past abuse, betrayal, words spoken in anger, abandonment, neglect, and a host of other negative recollections.

Perhaps now is the time to let is all go.

Assemble any pictures or any artifacts that tie you to those memories and throw them out. Burn them in a bonfire (while roasting marshmallows over the flames), or deliberately destroy each image in a shredder.

Remember, Christ made you a new creation. 2 Corinthians 5:17 states, "Therefore, if anyone is in Christ, the new creation has come: The old has gone, the new is here!"

Set it aside. Let it go. Don't look back. Allow joy to return to your heart.

Exercise

I am the absolute last person on earth to encourage people to exercise. For me, exercising is little more than an exercise in frustration. For countless others, it is the ticket to a happier life.

There is ample research to prove that moving your body makes you feel better.

There are lots benefits to taking time to exercise, including:

- Reducing chemicals in your system that cause depression.
- Decreasing feelings of anxiety.
- Helping to lower blood pressure.
- Producing chemicals and neurotransmitters in the brain that work to stimulate our minds, such as:
- Dopamine—Works to increase energy and produce feelings of exhilaration.

- Oxytocin—Boosts your immune system, increases problem-solving abilities, and produces feelings of calm and safety.
- Norepinephrine—Increases arousal and alertness, and greatly focuses attention.

More importantly, the act of exercising releases endorphins into your body. These little chemicals work to communicate with nerve cells throughout the body to relieve pain. Research shows endorphins are twenty to thirty times more powerful than morphine.

Endorphins produce a calming effect and create a sense of pleasure that reduces stress and boosts confidence. Consider it the antidote to stress, which tends to zap your joy.

Even if it is taking a walk, just getting outside and increasing your heart rate can do wonders not only physically, but mentally as well.

There is also something about walking at night that can really improve your life. Most adults are glued to screens all day. They turn off the TV and try to fall asleep. But the light from the screen works against your body's efforts to induce you to sleep.

Screen time keeps your brain fully engaged. It is processing sights and sounds as quickly as they are bombarding you.

The blue light emitted from electronic screens of any size work to prevent the development of melatonin, the hormone that stimulates sleep.

A brisk walk at night does several things. First, it gets the heart rate up to 185 beats per minutes, which also gives you an endorphin boost. Next, the darkness stimulates the production of melatonin, which prepares your body for sleep.

One of the things that contributes to a joyless existence is the lack of a good night's sleep. So, preparing your body for a refreshing rest—and removing distractions like the dinging of cell phones—enables your body to get the sleep it needs.

In turn, you'll wake up with a more positive outlook and a more joyful, grateful heart.

Remember Previous Victories

There were times in the past when things seemed hopeless and out-of-control. Yet, you survived. The rain stopped. The sun came out. And life returned to normal.

In order to keep your eyes focused on God—who is able to do immeasurably more than all we ask or imagine, according to his power that is at work within us (Ephesians 3:20)—sometimes we need to reflect on the many ways God came through for us in the past.

When you are surrounded by worry, doubt, fear and stress, it is nearly impossible to see any way out. Rest assured, God is already three steps ahead and working out the solution in your favor.

Using a journal (or even an online calendar), I like to record times of tremendous breakthrough, answered prayers, and situations when God came through for me in the past.

When it's on my calendar, then I get an annual reminder of that event. It pops up in the morning, and I'm reminded of that victory. "Oh, yeah," I'll say to myself. "I remember that hopeless night and the message God sent to me. He really did come through."

You may think a solution to some situation is impossible. But that's when God rolls up his sleeves and reminds us to watch what he's going to do next. He's not even going to work up a sweat.

Satan, the father of all lies, relishes in the opportunity to steal our joy and fill our minds with doom and gloom. The last thing he wants us to do is remember the many times God jumped into our mess and fixed it—even when we caused the problem ourselves.

I saw an interesting idea where someone wrote on a stone a description of every time God made a way in an impossible situation. They make great paperweights or decorations. Soon, you'll have enough to make a firm foundation for your life.

According to author John Eldredge,

Remembering when Jesus came through fertilizes our hope. It makes our faith burgeon and bloom. It strength-

ens our belief in the promises of God that He is good and He is for us. Remembering fuels our joy even when surrounded by thieves who want to steal it.

Sometimes being a joyful person amid this crazy world seems impossible. Well then, let the impossible commence. Because one of the secrets to being defiantly joyful is that it has absolutely nothing to do with the circumstances going on in your life or your world. Defiant joy does not depend on feeling happy.

Defiant joy is solely based on the victory of Jesus Christ and all that He has won for you. It rests on the fact that you are completely and utterly loved and cared for. In Christ your life is inextinguishable. Undefeatable. Victorious.

Worry, fear, panic, and dread do not get to hold your heart hostage in their viselike grip. Your heart is safely held in the hands of your faithful God who promises that a life of unending joy is your inheritance. It is coming. Jesus led the way. And though the way often includes disappointment, pain, betrayal, and sorrow, none of them get to have the final say.

Only God has the final say over your life. Your future is secure. Your Father is faithful. His promises are true.

Write down those victories and remember them often, especially when you don't see any options. Remember that you felt that way before, yet God came through for you in ways you never expected. Trust me, he's anxious to do it again.

Find a Hobby

A few years before my grandmother died, I had the opportunity to spend a considerable amount of time with her. She had always been one of my strongest cheerleaders. And, because I was her only grandson among six grandchildren, I always held a special place in her heart.

I was surprised to learn that my grandmother had experienced a nervous breakdown when she was in her early twenties that required hospitalization.

Let's just say that grandma had a hard life as a kid as she was shuttled from city to farm to one of the most remote places in Canada in the early 1900s. Worry and stress had consumed her thinking, and it was impacting her health and her life.

While she was sitting in the hospital, the doctor told her, "Betty, you have got to find a hobby that will take your mind off the worries of this life. Whether it is sewing or gardening, do it in silence and listen as God speaks to you."

So, my grandmother did both. She became exceptionally talented with her fingers by sewing clothes and quilts, crocheting, knitting, or cross-stitching some gift for one of us. She also learned to grow flowers and would carefully tend to her beautiful gardens.

She was always one of the most peaceful, joyful people I knew. She learned the secret that many people never discover.

Your mind is active all the time. It is either thinking positive thoughts or negative thoughts. Your mind is Satan's playground where he likes to be the neighborhood bully. If you're not using your mind to think positive, productive thoughts, he will immediately start filling it with doubt, fear, and anxiety.

Whether it is sewing, gardening, writing, golfing, fishing, crossword puzzles, real puzzles, walking, biking, working with wood (my grandfather's favorite), or engaging in something to occupy your mind, you'll consistently be pulled toward darkness.

Yes, it's important to be with people. But, it is also important to have a hobby you can enjoy by yourself whenever it is convenient. Slowing down and working with your hands means you're actively involved in the creation process. It also quiets your mind so you can hear God's still, soft whispers of love and reassurance.

Put an End to Procrastination

We all do it. Every day.

Starting as kids, we're often told to clean our rooms, which is often a monumental task for a kid. So we go to our rooms and are immediately distracted by dozens of shiny objects beckoning for our attention.

As adults, we have Facebook, news, television, video streaming, and, of course, the refrigerator to keep us from doing the one thing we know needs to be done.

Yet, when we procrastinate, rather than doing it, checking it off our to-do list, and feeling a sense of accomplishment, we start getting angry with ourselves. That's even more of a problem when we are under some type of deadline.

When you accomplish something, you'll feel much better.

So, at the start of every morning, write down just three things you want to accomplish that day. Then zero in on the most difficult challenge. Get it off your plate so it stops acting like a siren bombarding your brain.

Some people have found that ending their day by setting the top three priorities for the next day allows them to wake up and immediately get to work. By working early in the day, when you're fresh and full of energy, you can often accomplish more in three hours than you can the rest of the day.

Most of us set annual goals every December or January. Then we sit on them until November before we start working feverishly to complete them. Because we procrastinated instead of doing the work, we feel guilty and beat ourselves up for not meeting our goals.

In his book *The 12 Week Year*, author Brian Moran outlines a process that allows you to accomplish a year's worth of goals in just three months. I highly recommend the book.

I think his system can be modified even more to set monthly goals.

These short-term goals keep you focused like a laser on accomplishing your major goals.

Imagine accomplishing everything you were planning to do this year in thirty or ninety days!

When you accomplish a goal, you increase your confidence and self-esteem which, in turn, produces joy in your heart. Try it today.

Make a Friend

There is an old saying that suggests whenever you could really use a friend, you can't find one. Yet, when you want to be a friend, you'll find them everywhere.

In this era of social media and online communication, it seems that face-to-face relationships are becoming scarce. Even among younger people, the idea of "hanging out" with someone rather than texting is starting to take hold again.

We're called to relationships. Something deep inside hungers for connection with other people. You may not be able to pick your crazy relatives, but you certainly can pick your friends.

You'd be surprised what a plate of cookies will do to break the ice with a neighbor or coworker. You don't even have to entertain people in your own messy house. There seems to be a coffee shop on every corner these days.

As I've become older, I've sensed that people are lonelier today than they have ever been. We all like to be noticed and appreciated.

We also like to talk about ourselves. If you take a sincere interest in another person, you'll make a fast friend. And you don't have to go deep in conversation by baring your soul and revealing your greatest fears or unloading your current difficulties. Keep the conversation positive with questions like these:

- What's your favorite place to visit?
- What do people say you're really good at doing?
- What made you choose your career?
- How did you wind up in this community?
- If time or money wasn't a problem, what would you like to do?

Safe questions like that will open the door to fun, light conversations. You might never become best friends, but who knows? At least you will have made another friend and expanded your network of acquaintances.

Turn Off the Pornography

This may sound like an out-of-place suggestion, but I assure you it's not. According to recent statistics, two out of every three men and one out of every three women have a problem with pornography.

It's not something you typically do with other people. Therefore, pornography often leaves you isolated, feeling empty and certainly unfulfilled. For some, it brings back memories of abusive situations.

I wrote a book on the topic a few years ago titled Pornocide: Why Lust is Killing Your Faith, Stealing Your Joy and Destroying Your Life. It's a fictional story of a man caught in his sin. Through divine appointments, he meets people who strengthen his faith to the point that he can finally walk away.

Most people get hooked on porn because they turn to it to soothe feelings of abandonment, neglect, loneliness, fear, and uncertainty. But, viewing it often leaves people feeling more lonely, embarrassed, and guilty.

Trying to break an addiction to pornography leads to feelings of despair or anger for consistently caving into to the demands of their flesh. I guess you could say the same about any addiction.

When you cave in, it brings momentary pleasure, but that soon evaporates as you return to the same reality you were in before you turned to your empty self-indulgence.

An addiction to pornography is one of the worst I know. I have no research to back up my belief, but since much of the world seems on the boiling point of rage, I wonder if the proliferation of pornography has anything to do with it.

It's a slippery-slope addiction that takes you places you don't want to go, and from where it is very difficult to return.

John Bevere has an exceptional online course titled "Porn Free." You can access the affordable course at messengercourses.com.

Ending that habit will certainly bring joy to your life.

Conclusion

Yes, it is possible to restore joy to your life. It may not happen overnight, but if you are diligent to guard your thoughts and use them to guide your actions, you will be more joyful.

Joy is different from happiness: being happy is momentary. A gift can make you happy. An "A" on a test can make you happy. A job promotion can make you happy. New clothes, a new car, or a new house can make you happy. But it's a fleeting feeling.

Joy is a heart issue. It goes beyond momentary emotion to become a lifestyle.

Proverbs 4:19 warns us, "Above all else, guard your heart, for everything you do flows from it."

"To guard" is an active verb. It requires action on our part. It requires diligence to capture every thought that enters our mind and make it obey what we want to think about.

In Philippians 4:8, Apostle Paul encourages us with this reminder: "Finally, brothers and sisters, whatever is true, whatever is noble, whatever is right, whatever is pure, whatever is lovely, whatever is admirable—if anything is excellent or praiseworthy—think about such things."

Garbage in, garbage out. We can think about strife, injustice, famine, poverty, lack, need, politics, war, illness and a host of joy-squelching topics. Or we can focus our attention on the fruit of the Holy Spirit, which is love, joy, peace, patience, kindness, goodness, gentleness, faithfulness, and self-control.

One choice brings death. The other brings life.

Jesus warns us in John 10:10, "The thief (Satan) comes only to steal and kill and destroy; I have come that they may have life and have it to the full."

May your life be an abundance of peace, prosperity, good health, fulfilling relationships, memorable experiences, and, most of all, deeply-rooted joy.

About the Author

A native of Wisconsin, Greg Gerber is a DODO—Dad of Daughters Only—to three grown daughters. Growing up surrounded by girls, he speaks fluent female (although he struggles in the wife dialect).

A former journalist covering the recreation vehicle industry, he abandoned that in 2019 to pursue a career as a faith-based writer, public speaker, and coach.

He now lives in Arizona and still enjoys traveling, especially taking cruises. He has visited every state except Hawaii.

Hooked on pornography at age twelve and addicted to it for nearly forty years, in 2017 he wrote *Pornocide: How Lust is Killing Your Faith, Stealing Your Joy and Destroying Your Life*. He has also ghostwritten several other books.

Today, his mission is to ignite "bored-again" Christians and infuse them with knowledge of God's kingdom power to become passionate, productive disciples of Jesus Christ and to live life to the full.

Greg publishes a weekly faith-based newsletter titled Perspectives that offers unique insight to spiritual issues and current events.

You can contact him and subscribe to that free newsletter by visiting www.greggerber.com.

www.ingramcontent.com/pod-product-compliance
Lightning Source LLC
Chambersburg PA
CBHW061210070526
44583CB00025B/3189